Elon Musk

A Biography of an Entrepreneur

Joseph Greene

Table of Contents

Introduction

I don't ever give up. I'd have to be dead or completely incapacitated. – Elon Musk

Genius, billionaire, playboy, philanthropist.

A Tony Stark quotation from *The Avengers*? True, but also a concise description of Elon Musk, who inspired Robert Downey Jr in his creation of the Tony Stark character. But don't call him the real-life Tony Stark to his face. Or the next Steve Jobs. Musk hates being typecast. He is his own man, with his own aspirations, and he has shown that he is willing to break the mold to make his dreams a reality.

The 50-year-old South-African born entrepreneur, who overtook Amazon CEO Jeff Bezos as the world's richest man in May 2022, shot to fame when he founded SpaceX in 2002 and assumed the position of chief executive at Tesla in 2008.

Driven by idealism and the desire to be actively involved in the progression of humankind, Musk has been dubbed a "thrillionaire" by *The New York Times*; a tech entrepreneur using his wealth to turn science fiction into science fact.

Musk wants to save planet Earth, send civilians into space, and colonize Mars. He wants to create artificial intelligence that will aid humanity, and he wants to treat spinal and other neurological diseases and injuries by implanting computer chips in people's brains. His various businesses, such as the aforementioned Tesla and SpaceX, along with SolarCity (now Tesla Energy), Neuralink, OpenAI and Hyperloop, all work towards his goals.

This book aims to serve as a biography-to-date of this interesting entrepreneur. By the completion of this book, you will have a much clearer understanding of who exactly Elon Musk is, how he got to where he is, and what might be next for him!

Chapter 1: A Child of Africa

Elon Reeve Musk was born in Pretoria, South Africa, on June 28, 1971. His mother, Maye Musk, is a Canadian model and dietician. She appeared on the covers of numerous magazines, including Vogue. She was a finalist in the Miss South Africa beauty pageant in 1969, and married Musk's father, Errol, in 1970. Errol Musk is an electromechanical engineer. Errol is also a pilot, sailor, consultant, and property developer. At a time, Errol was the co-owner of an emerald mine in Zambia, and it is believed that this is from where the family's wealth was derived. Musk has a younger brother, Kimbal, and a sister, Tosca.

From a young age, Musk was described as being in another world in his mind. The boy was so quiet that his parents suspected that he was deaf. As an introverted child, Musk would rather spend his time reading than in the company of people.

Growing Up Segregated

Being white and wealthy in South Africa in the 1970's was to be in a position of great privilege. White-owned businesses prospered, and white South Africans had access to the best education available. The Musk family had all of this; a beautiful home in a safe neighborhood, good jobs with excellent salaries, and only the best education for their children.

Although the Musk family lived in an upper-class white suburb in Pretoria, their stance on apartheid was unlike that of their counterparts. Errol Musk was elected to the city council of Pretoria as a representative of the Progressive Party, one of the liberal political parties in apartheid South Africa. The family shared Errol's political views and had good relationships with black people.

Musk's parents divorced in 1980 and, at first, the children stayed with their mother. Elon felt sorry for his father because all his children had left him and he felt that the man was lonely, so he decided to live with him while his mother moved to Canada. Musk later regretted his decision and his relationship with his father became strained. Musk has alleged that his father was verbally abusive to him, telling the boy that he would never amount to anything. In an interview with *Rolling Stone* magazine, Musk said that his father was a truly evil human being, and eventually ceased having a relationship with him.

Computers Are the Future

At the age of 11, Musk was already interested in computers and wanted to learn more about them, instinctively knowing that they were the future. Errol enquired with regards to courses that his son could attend and found that the few that were available, were only for adults. Due to his son's persistence, Errol was able to book him a seat at the inaugural lecture hosted at the University of the Witwatersrand in Johannesburg. Musk was given clear instructions to sit down and keep quiet, as he was only in primary school at the time.

After the three-hour lecture, when Errol returned to collect his son, Musk was not in the lecture hall, but was in an in-depth discussion with the guest lecturers in one of the nearby offices. The guest lecturers were astounded by the young boy's passion and knowledge, and advised Errol that he should buy his son a computer as soon as possible. Luckily, Errol was able to purchase one with a discount and Musk was able to teach himself computer programming using a manual and the Disk Operating System (DOS).

By the age of 12, Musk had created a BASIC-based video game called *Blastar*. He sold the game to *PC and Office Technology* magazine for $500.

Educating a Genius

I was raised by books. Books, and then my parents.
–Elon Musk

Musk attended Waterkloof House Preparatory School in Pretoria, an English-medium all-boys private primary school. At the time, only white boys were allowed to attend. After completing his primary education, Musk briefly attended Bryanston High School in Johannesburg, before graduating from Pretoria Boys High School.

As a child, Musk was extremely introverted and always tended to be one of the smaller boys in his classes, which resulted in excessive bullying. One time, bullies pushed Musk down a flight of stairs and beat him until he passed out, resulting in his hospitalization. Around the age of 15, tired of the constant bullying, Musk began taking lessons in karate, judo, and wrestling. Along with a pubescent growth spurt that made him shoot up to around 6-feet tall, he was able to gain the confidence to stand up to the bullies.

Musk was not interested in mainstream school activities such as sports but rather, was a member of the computer club at Pretoria Boys High School. Musk graduated from Pretoria Boys

High School in 1988, with distinctions in Physical Science and Computer Science.

Goodbye, South Africa

When Musk graduated from high school in 1988, he was required to complete the compulsory military training that was put in place by the South African government. Musk refused to do so and decided to move to Canada, where his mother lived. He applied for his Canadian passport and while awaiting the documentation, he attended the University of Pretoria for five months. Being a university student was one of the ways that he could avoid doing his military service.

His passport arrived and, in June 1989, he moved to Saskatchewan, Canada. Before he left, his father told him that he would be back in South Africa in a few months, with his tail between his legs. Once in Canada, he lived with a cousin and worked odd jobs at a farm and a lumber mill. For a time, Musk also interned at the Bank of Nova Scotia.

Higher Learning

Musk enrolled at Queen's University in Ontario, Canada, in 1990, and studied there for two years before transferring to the University of Pennsylvania in Philadelphia. He earned a bachelor's degree in physics as well as a degree in economics from the Wharton School. Despite his busy workload, he was still able to have some fun. With the help of a fellow student, they rented a 10-bedroom fraternity house and then used it as a nightclub to help afford the rent. The shy boy from his childhood remained in South Africa, while the outgoing student flourished in the United States.

After completing his two bachelor's degrees, Musk was accepted into the distinguished doctoral program at Stanford University in California. Musk packed up and moved out West. His arrival in California in 1995 coincided with the dot com boom in Silicon Valley. In the summer prior to the start of his doctoral program, he was able to hold two internships in Silicon Valley. After attending Stanford for only two days, Musk dropped out to start his own company and seize the opportunities that the dot com boom could offer.

Chapter 2: The Entrepreneur Emerges

You should take the approach that you're wrong.
Your goal is to be less wrong. – Elon Musk

Musk's qualifications in physics and economics paved the way for his business ventures. His interest in computers from an early age and the Internet boom taking place in Silicon Valley allowed Musk to skyrocket into the world of Internet startups. However, the idealist in him has always wanted to make the world a better place, and this is where his background in physics allowed him to go above and beyond that of his peers.

Musk regularly speaks of the scientific method he uses to come up with ideas, solve a problem, or decide to start a company. He explains his scientific method as follows:

1. Ask a question
2. Gather as much evidence as you can
3. Develop hypotheses based on your evidence and assign the likelihood of truth to each one
4. Draw a conclusion about each hypothesis regarding their relevance
5. Try to disprove your own conclusion, and ask others to do the same
6. If your conclusion can't be disproved, you are probably right

Musk says that his scientific method is helpful for figuring out tricky situations but, unfortunately, most people prefer to use wishful thinking, and make decisions based on what others are doing.

Using the Dot Com Boom: Zip2

In 1995, with Greg Kouri, his brother Kimbal, and a $15,000 investment from a group of angel investors in Silicon Valley, Musk launched Global Link Information Network. Various sources state that Musk's father, Errol, also provided a portion of the startup capital, but Musk denied the statement, later stating that his father invested in the company at a later stage.

At the time, they were so strapped for cash that they were unable to afford an apartment. The brothers lived in the office space they rented, taking turns sleeping on a beat-up couch, and showering at the local YMCA.

Sharing a single computer, the brothers worked constantly. At first, Global Link assisted local businesses in attaining an Internet presence, by linking their services to search engines and providing directions, using the free Navteq database and a local business directory.

In 1996, Global Link received a $3 million investment and officially changed the business name to Zip2. Zip2's strategy changed; they would now sell software packages to newspapers, allowing them to build their own directories. Zip2's slogan "We Power the Press," was officially trademarked, and Musk was appointed Chief Technology Officer, with Rick Sorkin as CEO. They created an online city guide with maps, directions, and other information. Zip2 had a product called Auto Guide, which connected online newspaper users to vehicle dealerships or private car sellers.

The Musk brothers were quickly able to secure the *New York Times* and the *Chicago Tribune* as clients. By 1998, Zip2 had partnered with approximately 160 publications, developing city guides for them. In April of the same year, Musk attempted a merger with its main competitor, CitySearch. Although Musk initially accepted the offer to merge, it later failed due to incompatibilities in culture and technology.

In February 1999, Compaq bought Zip2 for $307 million in cash, to upgrade the Altavista search engine. As the original co-founders, Musk received a 7% share, equivalent to $22 million, while Kimbal received $15 million.

Banking Goes Online with X.com

During the 1990's, Musk had been toying with the idea of creating a full-service online bank, including checking and savings accounts, brokerages, and insurance. By 1999, he believed that people were ready to start using the Internet as their main bank.

The planning of X.com began while the sale of Zip2 was still in progress. Approximately one month after the sale was finalized, Musk invested $12 million and co-founded X.com with Harris Fricker, Christopher Payne, and Ed Ho as his business partners. Fricker was an ex-colleague from the Bank of Nova Scotia, Payne was a friend of Fricker's, and Ho was an executive at Zip2.

The company officially launched in December 1999. Customers were able to open an account online and send money using only the recipient's email address. Customers were not charged overdraft penalties or service fees, but instead received a $20 cash card upon signing up and a $10 card for referring new customers. This was a first in the banking industry, and within two months, they had signed up over 200,000 clients.

By March 2000, X.com merged with its closest competitor, Confinity. The merged companies operated under the X.com name, with Musk as its biggest shareholder and CEO. Confinity's main product was PayPal, which allowed users to transfer funds online.

Musk clashed with Confinity co-founder Peter Thiel over the use of Microsoft versus Unix software, resulting in Thiel's resignation. In September 2000, while Musk was in Australia, the board of directors ousted Musk and replaced him with Thiel as CEO. By June 2001, X.com was officially renamed PayPal. On October 3, 2002, PayPal was bought for $1.5 billion by eBay. Musk received $175.8 million as he was the biggest shareholder at the time with 11.72% of shares. Citing sentimental value, Musk purchased the domain X.com from PayPal in 2017 for an undisclosed amount.

To Infinity and Beyond with SpaceX

I think it would be great to be born on Earth and die on Mars. Just hopefully not at the point of impact. – Elon Musk

As a member of the Mars Society, a non-profit organization that encourages the continued investigation of sustaining life on Mars, Musk started envisioning "Mars Oasis" in 2001. The project aimed to set up an experimental greenhouse on Mars where plants could be grown from seed, using dehydrated gel. Musk believes that humanity's survival is limited if we remain a one-planet species.

Musk realized that even if he had a bigger budget than NASA, traveling to Mars would still be exorbitantly expensive if new rocket technology was not developed. In October of that year, Musk traveled to Russia with other entrepreneurs interested in revolutionizing space travel to purchase intercontinental ballistic missiles (ICBM's), which could be revamped to send payloads to Mars. Meetings were held with two companies: NPO Lavochkin and Kosmotras. Unfortunately, the Russians saw them as a group of amateurs and turned them away. The group returned to the United States empty-handed.

Musk returned to Russia in February 2002, with the same objective. He once again met with Kosmotras and they offered him an ICBM for $8 million. Musk rejected the offer as he felt it was too expensive. While on his return flight to the United States, Musk came to the realization that he could start a company to build the rockets he needed. By his calculations, the company would be able to produce rockets for a fraction of the cost.

In May 2002, Musk founded Space Exploration Technologies Corp., trading as SpaceX, using $100 million of his personal fortune. One of the goals of SpaceX was to create a rocket that could be used multiple times, making use of new and existing technologies, as well as keeping costs as low as possible. Musk began head-hunting inventors, technicians, and experienced engineers from Boeing and other similar companies, enticing them to join him at SpaceX's headquarters in El Segundo, California. Rocket engineer Tom Meuller joined the team early on and became SpaceX's Chief Technical Officer for Propulsion, a position he held until 2020.

In an effort to keep costs as low as possible, SpaceX began by building the smallest possible orbital rocket instead of a larger one, which would have bankrupted the company if it had failed.

As the company grew and developed the technology required, Musk set the deadline for their first launch to take place in November 2003, a mere 15 months from the company's inception. He also decided to name the first orbital launch vehicle Falcon 1, a nod to *Star Wars* and the Millennium

Falcon. The Falcon 1 would be only the third privately funded launch vehicle in history.

SpaceX bought approximately 10% of Surrey Satellite Technology in January 2005, and by 2006, Musk had invested over $100 million into SpaceX. In August 2008, SpaceX accepted an additional $20 million as an investment from Founders Fund, a San Francisco-based venture capital firm. By 2012, Musk owned approximately two-thirds of SpaceX, with his 70 million shares valued at $875 million.

The Falcon 1 cost between $90 and $100 million to develop, and the first two launches were purchased by the United States Department of Defense as part of a program evaluating new launch vehicles to be used by the Defense Advanced Research Projects Agency (DARPA). Falcon 1's maiden flight was canceled a number of times due to various technical issues and scheduling conflicts at the selected launch sites. The launch finally took place on March 24, 2006, in the Marshall Islands, but the flight ended after only one minute due to a leaky fuel line which resulted in a fire. The following two launches also ended in failure, almost resulting in the end of SpaceX. Musk was personally on the brink of bankruptcy due to financing problems for Tesla. Musk recalls that his stress levels were so high at the time that he was in continuous pain.

Despite the three failed launches, SpaceX was awarded a Commercial Resupply Services (CRS) program contract from NASA, after the fourth launch which was a success in 2008. The contract, along with a cash injection by Musk of $15 million, saved SpaceX's financial woes. The program's aim was to coordinate the development of vehicles to send crew and supplies to the International Space Station by the private sector. Due to her pivotal role in negotiating the contract with NASA, Gwynne Shotwell was promoted to company president.

After Falcon 1's fifth and final launch, SpaceX began to focus its attention on developing a bigger orbital rocket, known as the Falcon 9. The original plan had been to develop the Falcon 5, a medium capacity vehicle, but in 2005, it was decided to rather focus on the heavier Falcon 9. NASA agreed to purchase a number of commercial flights if certain requirements were met. The development of the Falcon 9 began in 2006, using money provided by the Commercial Orbital Transportation Services (COTS) program, a total of $278 million. The funding was to cover the development of the Dragon spacecraft and the Falcon 9 rocket, as well as demonstration launches of the two.

The Falcon 9 was first launched in June 2010, with a mockup of the Dragon spacecraft. The first fully operational Dragon spacecraft was launched in December 2010, marking Falcon 9's second flight. Dragon and Falcon completed two orbits around Earth and landed safely, successfully completing the mission's objectives. At the same time, SpaceX was manufacturing one Dragon and one Falcon every three months. In May 2012, Dragon would become the first commercial spacecraft to deliver supplies to the International Space Station. The success of the mission resulted in SpaceX's private equity value to almost double.

As part of the Commercial Crew Development (CCDev) program, NASA awarded SpaceX a $75 million contract in April 2011, to develop a launch escape system on Dragon. This would be done in preparation for Dragon to begin transporting a human crew to the International Space Station. In August 2012, NASA awarded SpaceX a Space Act Agreement to deliver an in-depth design of the crew transportation system.

In 2013, SpaceX launched its first commercial mission for a private customer, Intelsat, making it Falcon 9's seventh successful launch since 2010. By 2014, SpaceX had nearly 50%

of all available contracts worldwide. SpaceX was also able to begin competing with United Launch Alliance, who had, until then, a monopoly on the launch of military payloads.

In 2014, NASA awarded SpaceX the Commercial Crew Transportation Capability (CCtCap) contract, allowing them to finalize the development of their crew transportation system. The contract specified a number of technical milestones, crewed and un-crewed test flights, and six operational missions.

Falcon 9 suffered its first major failure during its seventh resupply mission to the International Space Station in June 2015. The CRS-7 exploded approximately two minutes into the flight due to a steel strut breaking off due to the force of the acceleration. This caused a breach, allowing high-pressure helium to escape into the low-pressure propellant tank.

Another failure with the Falcon 9 occurred in September 2016, when the rocket exploded while being filled with propellant for a standard pre-launch readiness test. The payload, valued at $200 million, was completely destroyed. The failure could not be considered as an unsuccessful flight, but operations halted for four months while SpaceX determined what had gone wrong. SpaceX resumed flights in January 2017.

In 2017, SpaceX reached a 45% global market share for commercial launch contracts, and by 2018, over 100 launches had been successfully completed. In 2019, SpaceX launched its Starship and StarLink projects. In order to free up finances, SpaceX cut their staff by 10%.

The initial production and testing of Starship prototypes took place in Florida and Texas in early 2019, with the entire operation moving over to the newly built South Texas launch site later that year. In May 2019, SpaceX successfully launched the first 60 StarLink satellites, beginning what would become the largest commercial satellite constellation.

SpaceX achieved a landmark launch in May 2020, sending NASA astronauts Doug Hurley and Bob Behnken into orbit on a Crew Dragon Spacecraft from the Kennedy Space Center in Florida. This made SpaceX the first ever private company to send astronauts to the International Space Station, and the first crewed orbital mission launch from US soil in 9 years.

In July 2021, SpaceX revealed a drone ship named A Shortfall of Gravitas. The ship, named after a spaceship in Iain M. Banks' series of science fiction novels, allowed for the recovery of first stage launch vehicles at sea, after boosting a spacecraft into orbit. By April 2022, SpaceX had conducted 18 successful rocket launches, most of which have been for StarLink, delivering internet-beaming satellites into orbit.

Going Electric with Tesla

Tesla Motors, named as an homage to inventor Nikola Tesla, is a clean energy automotive company based in Austin, Texas, founded in 2003 by Martin Eberhard and Marc Tarpenning. Eberhard and Tarpenning wanted to build on the success that General Motors had found with the EV1, its experimental electric car. Even though the General Motors program had only run for three years, and the EV1 was never released for public purchase, it was still considered a success from an engineering perspective.

February 2004 saw Musk investing $6.5 million in Tesla Motors, now Tesla Inc, using proceeds from the sale of PayPal. The investment made him the majority shareholder in the company, and he joined the board of directors. A 2009 lawsuit settlement agreement allowed Musk, Eberhard, and Tarpenning, along with Ian Wright and J.B. Straubel, to call themselves co-founders. Wright was the third employee at Tesla, joining a few months after its founding, and Straubel joined as Chief Technical Officer in May 2004.

Musk quickly took a more active role within Tesla, overseeing the design of the Roadster, although he wasn't very involved in other day-to-day activities. Tesla's objective was to create a top-of-the-range sports car for the early adopters to the electric vehicle technology, before developing more mainstream vehicles such as compacts and sedans. As product architect, Musk can also be attributed to the design of the full range of vehicles offered by Tesla.

The first Roadster prototype was displayed at a 350-person event at Barker Hangar in Santa Monica, on July 19, 2006. The Roadster was launched in 2008 and became the first electric car using lithium-ion batteries to be in continuous production. It could travel approximately 250 miles on a single charged battery with comparable acceleration and top speeds, and the battery could be recharged by plugging into any wall outlet. The Roadster was priced at around $100,000, pricing most interested buyers out of the market. Charging time was also an issue, with a 24 to 48 hour wait until the vehicle was fully charged.

The Roadster is also the first car to be launched into space. On February 6, 2018, it was carried by a Falcon Heavy test rocket, crossing the orbit of Mars. The vehicle's production was discontinued in 2012, although the development of the second-generation Roadster was announced in 2017.

In 2007, Eberhardt clashed with Musk and resigned as CEO of Tesla, but remained on the advisory board, with the title President of Technology. Michael Marks filled in as interim

CEO and Ze'ev Drori took over as the permanent replacement in October 2007. Drori is largely credited with transforming the Roadster into a viable product, as production had stagnated prior to his arrival.

In 2008, Eberhard and Tarpenning left Tesla completely, claiming that they had been forced out of the company. Musk became CEO and product architect in 2008 and dismissed a quarter of Tesla's staff. Eberhard sued Musk and Tesla in 2009, for libel and slander, among other issues. Eberhard alleged that the financial problems and delays surrounding the Roadster had been blamed on his leadership. Eberhard dropped the suit later the same year.

In June 2009, Tesla received a loan of $465 million from the United States Department of Energy, in order to support the development of the Model S sedan as well as the development of powertrain technology. By May 2013, Tesla had fully repaid the loan, including the $12 million interest.

In May 2010, Tesla bought a factory from Toyota in Fremont, California, and began production of the Model S sedan by October of the same year. On June 29, 2010, Tesla became a public company, becoming the first vehicle manufacturer to do so since Ford Motors in 1956.

Production of the Roadster was stopped in January 2012, and the Model S was launched in June 2012. Apart from being the world's best-selling plug-in electric car in both 2015 and 2016, the Model S has also won the following additional accolades: Motor Trend Car of the Year in 2013, World Green Car 2013, *Automobile* magazine's Car of the Year 2013, *Time* magazine's Best 25 Inventions of the Year 2012 award, and *Motor Trend's* Ultimate Car of the Year 2019.

In 2014, Tesla saw the release of a driver-assistance program called Tesla Autopilot, which was included in all vehicles shipped out as of September of the same year. Known as "hardware version 1," all cars included sensors, along with the software to support the program.

By 2015, Tesla began emerging in the energy storage market by launching the Tesla Powerwall and Tesla Powerpack battery packs. These battery packs were suitable for home and business use, respectively. Within a week of their launch, Tesla received an estimated $800 million in orders.

The Tesla Model X was designed using the Model S platform and is a midsize crossover SUV, released in September 2015. Within a year, it was the seventh highest selling plug-in electric vehicle. The Model 3 was unveiled in March 2016, and over 320,000 potential buyers paid deposits for the vehicle which began production in July 2017. The Model 3 was the cheapest Tesla vehicle to date, which made the company ramp up production. Despite various production issues, the Model 3 became the best-selling electric car and passed the 1 million units sold milestone in June 2021.

The Model Y was designed using the Model 3's platform and the two vehicles share a number of similar design concepts. The Model Y was launched in 2019 and deliveries began in 2020. Future projects for Tesla Motors include the second-generation Roadster, the Tesla Semi, and the Cybertruck.

When Tesla purchased SolarCity in 2016, the company officially entered into the solar power generation game. The two businesses were able to merge by taking Tesla's vehicle battery storage systems and joining them with SolarCity's solar panel installation systems to create the subsidiary known as Tesla Energy.

Tesla Motors officially became Tesla Inc. in 2017. The name change came about to reflect the changes that Tesla had been going through with regards to its product offering. The once electric vehicle manufacturing company now included battery energy storage systems and solar power generation in its repertoire.

In August 2018, Musk took to Twitter to voice his idea of taking Tesla private. The tweet resulted in share prices to skyrocket and ended up with a lawsuit brought on by the Securities and Exchange Commission (SEC).

The first Tesla Gigafactory opened in 2019, in Shanghai, China, making it the first car factory in China to be fully owned by a foreign company. Additional Gigafactories were built near Berlin, Germany, and in Texas. As of 2019, Musk was the longest-serving CEO of an automotive company on a global scale.

Between 2015 and 2020, Tesla acquired a number of smaller companies including Riviera Tool, Grohmann Engineering, Perbix, Compass Automation, Hibar Systems, and German ATW Automation. These companies were purchased in order to further grow Tesla's automation processes. Additionally, Tesla purchased Maxwell Technologies and SilLion to improve Tesla's expertise in battery technology. Grohmann Engineering was renamed Tesla Grohmann Automation, and along with Maxwell Technologies, operated as subsidiaries of Tesla. The remaining companies were absorbed by Tesla.

In 2020, Tesla reached its goal of building half a million cars and in 2021, Musk changed his title to "Technoking" while retaining the position of CEO.

Harnessing the Sun: SolarCity and Tesla Energy

In 2006, Musk's cousins, Lyndon and Peter Rive, co-founded SolarCity. Musk provided them with the concept as well as the initial capital to start the business and served as chairman of the board of directors. Based in Fremont, California, SolarCity leased, sold, and installed solar energy systems.

In 2008, SolarCity began introducing solar leases as one of their services. This allowed homeowners to lease rooftop solar panels at no cost upfront, then paying for the power generated for the next 20 years. This meant that homeowners would pay less than they had previously paid to municipal utility companies. Although the leasing model became SolarCity's most popular service in the United States, it also accounted for the majority of their debt, reaching over $3 billion in 2016.

SolarCity completed a number of large-scale installations for businesses in 2008 and 2009. The client list included eBay's North Campus in San Jose, California, British Motor Car Distributors in San Francisco, Walmart, Intel, as well as the US military.

In 2011, SolarCity expanded their operations to the US East Coast by buying the solar division of Clean Currents and groSolar. SolarCity was then able to provide services to Connecticut, Pennsylvania, South Carolina, Florida, Vermont, and New Hampshire.

In 2013, SolarCity became the second largest solar systems provider in the United States. In the same year, SolarCity bought Paramount Solar for $120 million, and by 2015, they were responsible for over 25% of non-utility installations in the United States.

In 2014, SolarCity announced plans to construct a new factory in Buffalo, New York, in partnership with the State University of New York Polytechnic Institute. The factory, known as Gigafactory 2, would be the largest of its kind in the Western Hemisphere. Construction began in September 2014, with an estimated completion date of 2016. Due to delays with machinery, the factory didn't begin production until the summer of 2017.

SolarCity offered $200 million in stocks in its first public offering in 2014, and in 2015, SpaceX purchased $90 million in SolarCity stock. Also, in 2015, SolarCity withdrew its services from the state of Nevada due to the state's restrictions on selling solar energy back to the grid. This resulted in scrapping over 500 jobs in Nevada.

The headcount at SolarCity had grown so rapidly in 2015 that the company cut 20% of jobs in 2016, across all sectors of the business, in an effort to cut costs. Operations, manufacturing, and installations suffered a 22% drop in headcount, while the sales and marketing departments lost 27% of their staff. Co-founders, the Rive brothers, also had their salaries cut from $275,000 to only $1 per annum.

In August 2016, Tesla announced its acquisition of the entirety of SolarCity's stock valued at $2.6 billion, resulting in a marked increase in Tesla's value. The acquisition would further Tesla's aim of accelerating the shift to renewable energy. Once production began at Gigacity 2, Musk announced that all Tesla solar roof products would be moved to the facility by the end of 2017.

After Tesla's acquisition of SolarCity, the newly named Tesla Energy changed the original business model to incorporate Tesla's own interests. Tesla Energy moved to mainly residential solar panel installations, with a few commercial customers based in California. SolarCity's lease program was discontinued in order to curb the debt incurred. Tesla Energy announced the Tesla Solar Roof in 2016, which it manufactures, installs, and sells. Tesla Energy claimed that the solar shingle is both cheaper and more durable than a regular roofing tile.

SolarCity Chief Policy Officer, John Wellinghoff, left SolarCity in April 2017. In June of the same year, co-founder Lyndon Rive left SolarCity, and was soon followed by his brother Peter.

Building on the technology created for electric car inverters, Tesla Energy launched its solar inverter in January 2021. Like the inverters on Tesla vehicles, they are able to receive over-the-air updates with cell phone connectivity. In order to keep costs as low as possible, the inverters are produced using string inverter technology, which is much older.

Tesla Energy has also developed and manufactured the Tesla Powerpack, which was launched in 2012; the Tesla Powerwall and MegaPack, launched in 2015 and 2019, respectively, and a software ecosystem developed to support its hardware products; namely Autobidder, Powerhub, Opticaster, Microgrid Controller and Virtual Machine Mode.

In July 2021, the Virtual Power Plant program was launched, allowing residential California Powerwall customers to send surplus power generated back to the grid during peak usage periods. The aim is to reduce the need for energy generated by fossil fuels.

The Future of the Human Mind: Neuralink

I think it is possible for ordinary people to choose to be extraordinary. – Elon Musk

In 2016, Neuralink was co-founded by Musk, Max Hodak, Ben Rapoport, Dongjin Seo, Paul Merolla, Philip Sabes, Tim Gardner, Tim Hanson, and Vanessa Tolosa. The neurotechnology company develops brain-machine interfaces (BMI's) that are implantable. The co-founders are all considered experts in robotics, neuroscience, and biochemistry. The company has also hired a number of neuroscientists from high-profile universities. The aim of Neuralink is to produce devices that can treat brain diseases in the short-term, eventually aiming for human enhancement, also known as transhumanism. Musk was inspired by the fictional world of *The Culture* by Iain M. Banks.

Musk has stated that artificial intelligence poses a threat to humanity, and through Neuralink, he hopes to attain symbiosis between the two. He wants the BMI device to be similar to a video game, where a person can pick up from a certain checkpoint, while at the same time addressing any neural injuries. Although Musk is a majority shareholder at Neuralink, he does not hold an executive position.

In 2018, it was reported that Neuralink was extremely secretive about its work. Public records do show, however, that Neuralink was looking to open an animal testing facility in San Francisco. The team at Neuralink began conducting testing at the University of California, Davis. This has been widely criticized by many animal rights groups, including PETA. The first prototype was revealed to the public at the California Academy of Sciences in 2019.

Neuralink has received criticism regarding their claims, with the *MIT Technology Review* stating that Musk's presentations only stir excitement and build a fanbase like that of SpaceX and Tesla. The publication has criticized Musk for holding product demonstrations while Neuralink has no products available to the public.

As of August 2020, only three of the co-founders remain with Neuralink. The reason for the departure of over half of the eight co-founders has been attributed to tight deadlines despite the slow progress of science.

Speeding up Travel with the Boring Company

With the aim of alleviating the traffic situation in Los Angeles, Musk founded The Boring Company (TBC) in December 2016. TBC constructs underground tunnels with the aim of designing intra-city transit systems, also known as loops. TBC was initially founded as a subsidiary of SpaceX but became an independent company in 2018. Musk has stated that TBC occupies only 2-3% of his time, so the business feels more like a hobby to him.

By February 2017, TBC announced that it would construct a testing tunnel under the SpaceX premises in Hawthorne, Los Angeles. In May, a tunnel boring machine with TBC branding on it arrived at the SpaceX premises. The machine was named Godot, in honor of the Samuel Beckett play, *Waiting for Godot*. All other TBC tunnel boring machines would be named after plays and poems. In November 2017, TBC filed an application with the Los Angeles city government to build a tunnel from Hawthorne to Westwood, along Interstate 405. The trip normally takes approximately 45 minutes in normal traffic. By placing cars on an electric sled and traveling at 120 miles per hour, the same trip would take only five minutes.

At the same time, TBC announced a Hyperloop project consisting of a sealed underground tunnel which would link New York City and Washington D.C. Musk stated that it would take less than 30 minutes to travel from one city to another. TBC adjusted its plans in March 2018, with Musk stating on Twitter that pedestrians and cyclists would be given priority, and that cars would be considered after all other mass transportation needs had been met.

In 2018, TBC began offering customers promotional materials, including hats, fire extinguishers, and, most infamously, a flamethrower inspired by 1987's *Spaceballs*, directed by Mel Brooks. The idea behind the sale of these promotional items was to generate some quick income for TBC, allowing it to use the funds for their upcoming projects.

The hats sold out in January 2018, creating $1 million in profits for TBC. TBC then began offering flamethrowers, which was a blowtorch modified to look like a gun. Despite huge criticism, the 20,000 flamethrowers were sold out in only 100 hours and brought in $10 million of profit to TBC. Maryland was excluded from the offer as such an item was illegal there. California State assemblyman Michael Santiago sought to introduce legislation to ban the flamethrower in California.

When customs officials announced that they would not allow passengers carrying flamethrowers onto flights, Musk renamed the product to "Not-A-Flamethrower," and claimed it was the world's safest flamethrower on the TBC website. A pick-up party for the not-flamethrowers was arranged, which included food trucks and a mariachi band. Buyers who were unable to collect their not-flamethrowers encountered challenges with delivery companies such as UPS, so Musk advised that they would be delivered by TBC employees. TBC then announced that fire extinguishers would be available to purchase. Musk stated that the extinguishers were very normal and also overpriced, but that they came with a cool TBC sticker.

In March 2019, the Las Vegas Convention and Visitors Authority (LVCVA) requested that TBC construct a tunnel to shuttle visitors underneath the Las Vegas Convention Center, with a completion date set for 2021. The LVCVA also highlighted the potential for expansion to include the Las Vegas Strip, the Allegiant Stadium, and McCarran International Airport. In December 2020, an additional expansion was requested to include Flamingo, Paris Las Vegas, the High Roller, Planet Hollywood, and Bally's, which would be known as Caesar's Loop.

In November 2019, Steve Davis became president of TBC after leading the company on behalf of Musk since 2016. Davis was one of the first engineers hired at SpaceX and he holds degrees in both particle physics and aerospace engineering.

TBC launched a tunnel-boring competition, named Not-A-Boring Competition, in 2020, with the final event taking place in Las Vegas, Nevada, in September 2021. The aim was to introduce innovative concepts to boring tunnels and increase the pace thereof. Almost 400 teams entered the competition by submitting their plans which went through an intense technical review process, resulting in the selection of 12 finalists.

The final challenge was to drill a 98-feet long tunnel with a 19.6 inch width as quickly and accurately as possible. After the safety briefing, it was found that only 2 of the 12 teams met all the requirements to tunnel the entire stretch, while the remaining teams were limited to shorter distances. The team from the Technical University of Munich (TUM) worked on their concept for over a year and were awarded the prize for Best Guidance System along with overall first place.

Similar to Neuralink, TBC, and Musk have been criticized for over-promising and under-delivering. The proposed tunnels in Los Angeles, Chicago, and Baltimore have never really broken ground, with TBC removing them from their list of upcoming projects. Civil engineering experts have doubted TBC's ability to bore tunnels more quickly and at a lower cost than their competitors, as there are no signs of new or improved technology in their technique.

While TBC's tunnels allow for the transportation of a maximum of four people in a Tesla at a time, a project to improve the Los Angeles Metro system features full-sized trains that can carry hundreds of passengers at a time. It's issues like this that make experts question the validity of TBC and its mission.

Twitter Take-Over

Musk has been an active Twitter user since creating his account in June 2010 and has since gained over 80-million followers. He uses the platform to post memes, promote his business ventures, and also to comment on political issues and social causes. Musk has criticized Twitter's commitment to free speech in the past and had previously stated that he was thinking of creating a rival platform.

Musk first expressed an interest in buying Twitter as early as 2017. One of his followers suggested the idea to Musk on the platform itself and Musk responded by asking, "How much is it?"

From January 2022, he began buying Twitter shares and by April had accumulated over 9% of shares in the social media platform, making him Twitter's biggest shareholder. Musk allegedly didn't file the paperwork required by the Securities and Exchange Commission (SEC) to advise of his share in the company. The SEC requires all individuals to notify when their share in a company is over 5% within 10 days. When Musk's investment in Twitter was publicly announced, a spurt of trading pushed Twitter's share price up by 27%. This superseded the trading that took place during Twitter's initial public offering in 2013.

Musk started bad-mouthing Twitter in March 2022, by asking his followers if the platform truly upheld the principle of free speech. Musk then met with co-founder and former CEO, Jack Dorsey, to talk about joining Twitter's board of directors. Dorsey passed the message on to Bret Taylor, chairman of Twitter, and CEO Parag Agrawal. The proposal from Musk was to either make Twitter a private company, or that he would create a rival social media platform.

In April 2022, Musk was invited to join the Twitter board of directors, an offer which he initially accepted. Agrawal stated that he was certain that Musk's place on the board would bring long-term value to the company. Dorsey stated that Musk cared deeply about Twitter and the role that it plays in our world.

Musk's position as a board member would have limited him from acquiring anything more than a 14.9% stake in the business, so four days before he joined the board, he rescinded his acceptance. Later that month, Musk made an offer to purchase Twitter for $43-billion and take the company private. The board of directors saw this as an attempted hostile takeover. Musk stated that he believed that Twitter had the potential to promote free speech on a worldwide scale and insisted that he had made the offer without the desire to increase his wealth.

The offer to purchase was met with both praise and criticism. Twitter employees were concerned about Musk's opinions on free speech, while those in the media expressed their concerns that Musk's proposed changes to the platform would result in misinformation and harassment of those who had differing opinions. Conservative Republicans in the United States were enthusiastic about Musk's proposed changes as they felt they had been silenced by Twitter from expressing their views on the platform.

On April 17, Taylor met with a number of Twitter's largest shareholders and was encouraged to take Musk's offer seriously. Three days later, Musk announced that he had obtained financing to purchase Twitter from Morgan Stanley, Bank of America, Barclays, MUFG, Société Générale, Mizuho Bank, and BNP Paribas. The financing was made up of senior secured bank loans, subordinated debt, personal bank loans to Musk himself using Tesla stock as security, cash equity from Musk, and equity from a number of independent investors.

On April 23, Musk met with Taylor and prompted him to accept the offer. A number of media sources began announcing that Musk and Twitter were in final negotiations, while Reuters stated that the deal could still fall through. The board of directors accepted Musk's offer on April 25, 2022, by unanimous vote. Twitter will become a private company once the transaction is completed. If Musk backs out of the deal, he will be required to pay a $1-billion breakup fee. Although Musk has already selected a replacement CEO to step in once the deal is complete, it's believed that he will serve as CEO until the replacement steps in.

Upon acceptance of Musk's offer, Twitter prohibited him from making negative remarks about them on the platform. Musk has not upheld this part of the deal by tweeting numerous critical remarks about many Twitter executives, including Vijaya Gadde, Twitter's Chief Legal Advisor.

Musk has announced that he will make Twitter's algorithm freely available to the public in order to increase the transparency of the business. He also wants to eradicate spambots to ensure that only real humans use the platform.

Agrawal addressed Twitter employees on April 29, to tackle any concerns that they had, and assured them that no one would lose their jobs. Republican politicians like Jim Jordan, Yvette Herrell, Marsha Blackburn, and Ted Cruz, lauded the deal, and called it a restoration of free speech. Democrat politicians, such as Pramila Jayapal, Jesús García, Marie Newman, Mark Pocan, and Elizabeth Warren, on the other hand, were highly critical of the acquisition, stating that the money used to finance the deal could have been used for philanthropic purposes.

Chapter 3: The Not-So-Private Life of a Genius

If I'm not in love, if I'm not with a long-term companion, I cannot be happy. – Elon Musk

It's easy to look at Elon Musk's life and summarize it in terms of his business ventures. But his businesses are not the only thing that puts Musk in the headlines. From young love and messy divorces to high-profile relationships and unpronounceable baby names, Musk has captured pop culture's imagination far more than any other billionaire to date.

Young Love Doesn't Last

Musk met Justine Wilson, a Canadian author, while they were both attending Queen's University in Ontario, Canada. Justine was born and grew up in Peterborough, Ontario, a relatively small city. In her first year at Queen's University, Justine was mourning a breakup with a much older boyfriend, who she described as Romeo in a dark-brown leather jacket. Musk was the complete opposite; clean-cut, studious, and upper-class.

Although Justine, an aspiring writer at the time, was not the only girl that Musk was pursuing at the time, he maintained communications with her after he transferred to the University of Pennsylvania, regularly sending her roses. When he returned to Canada to visit some friends at Queen's University, she agreed to have dinner with him. When she told him of her dream of being an author, he was impressed and supportive.

Justine felt that for the first time in her life, her ambition was taken seriously.

Musk and Justine spent a few years apart. Musk was in California building Zip2, while Justine taught English in Japan, before returning to Canada to work on her novel and bartending to pay the bills. Justine remembers telling her sister one night, "If Elon ever calls me again, I think I'll go for it. I might have missed something there." Musk phoned her a week later.

Musk had sold Zip2 the year prior and Justine found herself dating a very wealthy man while she was still a struggling writer. He bought a condo, a McLaren F1, and a plane. After their engagement, Musk scheduled a meeting with a lawyer to put together a financial agreement between the two, allegedly supported by the board of X.com.

According to Justine, "Elon's wealth seemed abstract and unreal, a string of zeros that existed in some strange space of its own."

The couple married in January 2020 and signed a postnuptial agreement two months later. Although she didn't know it at the time, the agreement restricted Justine from speaking about her new husband's business ventures in public. Growing up in South Africa's male-dominated culture, Musk quickly established himself as the alpha in the marriage. On more than one occasion, Musk told his wife that if she were his employee, he would fire her.

In 2002, the couple moved to Los Angeles and their first son, Nevada Alexander, was born. At 10 weeks old, after being put down for a nap, the infant stopped breathing. He was resuscitated by paramedics and was on life support for three days, but he was brain dead. His parents made the decision to take him off life support and he passed away in his mother's arms. The baby's death created a further rift between Musk and Justine. He refused to talk about what had happened, while she was openly grieving the loss of her baby. Within 2 months of Nevada's death, the couple visited an IVF clinic, hoping to become pregnant as soon as possible. In the space of five years, the couple had a set of twins, followed by a set of triplets.

Despite two successful pregnancies and five healthy baby boys, Justine was still deeply grieving the loss of her first-born son. Not even the publication of three of her novels was able to lift her from her depression. Musk apparently didn't notice, and it was one of the boys' nannies that approached Justine and suggested the name of an esteemed therapist. Despite being skeptical, Justine made her first appointment, and soon enough, she began to feel the dark veil of depression lift, and she began seeing her life from a new perspective.

From the outside, the couple lived a perfect life. The family lived in a mansion in Bel Air and had a domestic staff of five to help them with their everyday lives. In the evenings, the couple attended black-tie events, ate at the best restaurants, and partied next to Hollywood celebrities at the trendiest clubs.

Behind closed doors, it was a different story. Justine felt lonely in her marriage; even when he was home, Musk was constantly thinking about work. Justine felt that she was sacrificing a normal family life for his career. At the same time, Musk would place her every minor flaw under a magnifying lens, leaving her feeling inconsequential. According to Justine, they argued almost constantly, and the strain affected their five young sons.

After a car accident in 2008, Justine realized that something needed to change. She realized that she didn't recognize herself anymore; she had become the stereotypical trophy wife, and she wasn't even good at it. Justine felt that she couldn't keep a perfect home or be a decent hostess; she was bored by the superficial chit-chat at events; she had no interest in making herself look younger with make-up or Botox. She felt like she would never be the wife that Musk wanted her to be, nor did she even want to try any more.

Justine discussed her feelings with Musk, stating that she wanted equality in their marriage. Soon after, the couple started attending counseling sessions. After only three sessions, Musk filed for a divorce. Two years after their separation, the divorce was finalized. The couple are no longer in contact although they do share custody of their five sons.

According to Musk, "My children didn't choose to be born, I chose to have children. They owe me nothing, I owe them everything".

On-Again, Off-Again

While on a trip to London with a SpaceX investor in 2008, Musk met English actress Talulah Riley in a bar. The pair bonded immediately and spent four days together in London before Musk returned to Los Angeles. Talulah accompanied him and a mere 10 days later, Musk proposed. Musk had been single for a mere six weeks since his divorce from his first wife Justine. Talulah had no qualms with the speed at which their relationship was progressing. Her parents had become engaged very early in their relationship, with her father asking her mother to marry him at the end of their first date. She always felt that if someone wanted to marry her, they would want to do so immediately.

The couple got married in September 2010, in Scotland. The couple spent a few months apart in an attempt to rekindle their romance, but by 2012, they divorced. Musk expressed his love for Talulah on Twitter, but stated that after four years together, he had simply fallen out of love with her.

The couple stayed friends and remarried in 2013, only 18 months after their divorce. Their second marriage did not last long, and Musk filed for divorce in 2014. He withdrew the petition for divorce seven months later.

The reconciliation was temporary as Talulah filed for divorce in 2016. The couple have remained good friends and see each other occasionally.

Whirlwind Hollywood Romance

Musk met Amber Heard in 2013 on the set of *Machete Kills*, where he had a cameo appearance. They became good friends and would talk regularly. After their divorces from Talulah Riley and Johnny Depp respectively, Musk and Amber were spotted spending time together. Depp, however, believes that Musk and Amber had been having an affair before their marriage ended. Both Musk and Amber have denied the allegations.

On April 24, 2017, Amber posted a photo of herself and Musk, making their relationship Instagram official. By August of the same year, the couple announced their split, citing bad timing. Musk was extremely busy with his work at Tesla and SpaceX, while Amber was in Australia filming a movie. Five months later, they reconciled, only to split up once more in February 2018.

It's a Little Complicated

Musk began talking to musician Grimes on Twitter in 2018, when she replied to one of his tweets, making a pun about artificial intelligence. Grimes, also known as Claire Boucher, is also a music producer and unreserved advocate for women's rights, especially in the music industry. The pair met in person and began dating in secret for a few weeks before their relationship went public. Their first official outing as a couple was at the 2018 Met Gala.

The couple's relationship captured the public's interest due to their Twitter exchanges. Grimes has even defended Musk on the platform with regards to the unionizing of Tesla staff and donations to the Republican party made by Musk.

Grimes announced her pregnancy with Musk's baby in January 2020, via an Instagram post showing off her baby bump. Later, on Twitter, Musk revealed the baby's name as X Æ A-Xii, with Grimes providing an explanation to the name as follows: X is the unknown variable, Æ is the elven spelling of love (or stands for artificial intelligence), and A-Xii is the forerunner of the couple's favorite aircraft, which has no weapons and is non-lethal. The baby, a son, was born in May 2020, and is referred to as X.

After the birth of X, the couple's relationship deteriorated. Since September 2021, a variety of statements have been released by the couple with regards to their relationship, from them being semi-separated, to broken up, to "it's complicated." Musk and Grimes welcomed a baby daughter in December 2021, via surrogate, named Exa Dark Sideræl Musk, also known as Y.

To date, the couple remains separated, but on good terms. Grimes has revealed that she and Musk want to have more children together and, although they live apart, they see each other often and consider themselves best friends.

A Stab at Music

After the killing of Harambe, a gorilla at the Cincinnati Zoo in 2016, Musk released a track titled "RIP Harambe" on March 30, 2019. Musk released the track by sharing a link to SoundCloud. The song was a protest towards the killing and the online sensationalism thereafter. The track was performed by Yung Jake, with Musk providing additional vocals, and was produced by BloodPop.

On January 30, 2020, Musk released "Don't Doubt Ur Vibe," an EDM track featuring his own vocals and lyrics, via SoundCloud. Reviews of the track are mixed, with the *Guardian* calling it indistinguishable, to *TechCrunch* staging that it's a decent representation of the EDM genre.

There's Always Time to Relax

With the number of business ventures that Musk is involved in, and co-parenting seven children, it's safe to say that he does not have much spare time. He does, however, have a few hobbies that he partakes in despite his busy schedule.

Musk has been a gamer since childhood, citing gaming as the reason he became interested in computers and technology. Via Twitter, he has endorsed a number of games including *Cyberpunk 2077, Halo,* and *Mass Effect.*

Musk does take some time to disconnect in front of the TV, citing *Silicon Valley* and *Black Mirror* as his two favorite shows to binge-watch. Musk is a huge fan of historical documentaries, and he also loves anime. He has expressed his admiration for *Spirited Away* and *Princess Mononoke.* Musk has also appeared in cameos in TV series and movies, including *The*

Simpsons, The Big Bang Theory, Machete Kills, and *Iron Man 2.* In 2021, he hosted *Saturday Night Live.*

Musk has been an avid reader since childhood and loves fantasy, science-fiction, and biographies. He has stated that his favorite book is *The Lord of the Rings.* He also enjoys reading specialized books, for example, he loves reading about the Napoleonic wars, the evolution of aeronautic design, and structural engineering.

According to Musk, "The idea of lying on a beach as my main thing just sounds like the worst. It sounds horrible to me. I would go bonkers. I would have to be on serious drugs. I'd be super-duper bored. I like high intensity".

Chapter 4: The Gift of Giving

I'm not trying to be anyone's savior. I'm just trying to think about the future and not be sad. – Elon Musk

Philanthropy is part and parcel of being a billionaire, although some are more vocal about their charitable works than others. The Musk Foundation, founded by the Musk brothers in 2002, provides grants supporting renewable energy research, space exploration research, pediatric research, science and engineering education, and the development of safe artificial intelligence. The Musk brothers are the only two officers at the foundation and neither of them receives compensation for their work at the foundation. When the foundation was founded, Elon put in $2.1 million.

The foundation's mission remains obscure, but documentation has shown that the grants provided far supersede the scope provided. Some grants have gone into Musk's own business ventures, and those of his family, but Musk has also used the foundation to address some of his own passion projects. To date, the foundation has provided more grants to artificial intelligence research than to any of the other charitable causes it supports.

Charity Begins at Home

In the early years of the Musk Foundation, donations were given to the schools that Musk had attended, both in South Africa and in the United States. Other beneficiaries included other educational institutions, space societies, and children's hospitals in Los Angeles and Seattle.

Between 2007 and 2014, Musk added $3.1 million to the foundation's pockets. The list of beneficiaries grew and included organizations linked to Musk and his family. In 2010, the foundation provided funds to assist the victims of the Deepwater Horizon disaster, and in 2011, relief was provided to those affected by the Fukushima earthquake in Japan. In 2010, the foundation also donated over $180,000 to aid in launching Kitchen Community, a charity headed by Kimbal Musk based in Arizona. Kitchen Community creates gardens in unused areas where children can learn to grow and prepare food. Between 2010 and 2014, Kitchen Community received almost $500,000 from the Musk Foundation.

Between 2011 and 2013, the Musk foundation made numerous donations to his sons' school, the Mirman School for Gifted Children in Los Angeles. Musk then founded a non-profit school, Ad Astra, based at SpaceX headquarters in Hawthorne, which his sons now attend.

The Giving Pledge

Founded in 2010 by Bill Gates and Warren Buffet, The Giving Pledge is a campaign to encourage the vastly wealthy to donate the majority of their wealth to charitable causes, either during their lifetimes or upon their death. Musk signed the pledge in 2012.

Giving to Personal Interests

One of Musk's pet peeves has always been the traffic situation in Los Angeles, resulting in his founding of The Boring Company to create underground tunnels that will alleviate traffic congestion in the city. The Musk Foundation donated $75,000 to Angelenos Against Gridlock, a small group lobbying for the upgrade of Interstate 405.

Musk has had a long-running concern regarding the rise of malignant artificial intelligence and, in 2015, he pledged $1 billion to help set up OpenAI, a research organization that would develop 'safe' artificial intelligence with the aim of benefiting humanity.

There's Always Some Controversy

In 2016, the Musk Foundation donated over $37 million to Vanguard Charitable, a charity organization that collects and distributes donations on behalf of clients, making it challenging to know the source of the donation. Although secrecy has never been a cause for concern for Musk, he does believe that true philanthropy should be done anonymously.

The Musk Foundation's contributions to personal projects and interests, such as donating to his children's schools, have also caused some controversy for Musk. Harvey Dale, director of the National Center on Philanthropy and the Law at New York University, states that these donations are not atypical. Many billionaires have been known to support their own initiatives, especially through a private foundation.

Chapter 5: No Such Thing as Bad Publicity

Constantly seek criticism. A well thought out critique of whatever you're doing is as valuable as gold. – Elon Musk

Musk has been a frequent Twitter user since creating his account in 2010. More than once has he landed in hot water as he aired his views or made statements on the platform. Through his businesses and charitable works, he has also faced scrutiny, sometimes leading to legal proceedings.

Taking Tesla Private

The Securities and Exchange Commission (SEC) sued Musk in September 2018 as a result of a tweet where he announced that he had secured funding to buy the entirety of Tesla's shares. Due to the tweet, Tesla's share price skyrocketed. The Tesla board members were dumbfounded by the tweet, as there had been no discussions with investment banks to assist in the process of raising funds to take Tesla private. Tesla investors at that time also stated that they had not had such discussions with Musk.

The SEC claimed that the tweet was misleading to investors and sought to prohibit Musk from serving as CEO or director of any public company. This is the harshest punishment that the SEC can enforce on any executive.

The case between Musk and the SEC was settled, however Musk refused to acknowledge any wrongdoing. The SEC fined both

Musk and Tesla $20 million each and Musk had to step down from the board of directors for three years.

When Musk took to Twitter in 2019 to state that Tesla would build half a million cars that year, the SEC stepped in and filed in court. The SEC stated that the tweet violated the terms of the settlement agreement the year before. The case was once again settled, and the agreement included a list of topics that Musk would require clearance prior to tweeting about.

Should We Follow the Leader?

Musk's leadership and managerial style has been criticized throughout his career. He is both a genius and a workaholic, resulting in demanding and gratifying experiences for his staff. Lately, Musk has been observed as displaying much more haphazard behavior in the workplace, with Tesla board members being concerned about his recreational use of Ambien, usually used to treat sleeping issues.

Musk has been known to throw mercurial fits at Tesla, with employees being warned to stay away from him, as he would randomly fire anyone within his range. He's also been known to change the direction of the business in an instant, based on the changing trends he found in social media. All of this has led to a high turnover of staff, especially those in more senior positions.

A number of senior engineers left Tesla after Musk insisted on marketing the vehicles as self-driving. One engineer stated that Musk's decision was reckless and would put customer's lives at huge risk. Between 2018 and 2022, a total of five senior members in Tesla's legal department have left, as well as an undisclosed number of lower-level lawyers.

An article in *Business Insider* alleges that SpaceX paid one of its flight attendants $250,000 with regards to a sexual misconduct allegation in 2018. The flight attendant worked for SpaceX's corporate jet fleet and alleged that in 2016, Musk exposed himself to her, touched her without her consent, and offered her gifts in exchange for a full body erotic massage. The flight attendant alleges that her schedule was decreased significantly after declining Musk's offer. Musk declined the allegation and stated that the story was a "politically motivated hit piece".

Allegations of sexual harassment have been brought against Tesla, although not against Musk himself. In 2021, seven female staff members spoke up about sexual harassment and discrimination.

Musk to the Rescue

On June 23, 2018, a junior football team entered the Tham Luang Nang Non cave in Chiang Rai Province in northern Thailand, after the team's practice session. After a flash flood, signaling the early start of the monsoon season, the twelve team members, aged 11 to 16, and their 25-year-old assistant coach were trapped in the flooded cave. The incident garnered international interest, and a number of countries provided assistance to the rescue mission.

In July 2018, the boys had been trapped in the cave for over a week after several failed rescue attempts. Musk asked a group of employees to build a mini submarine to assist in the rescue, requested by the leader of the international rescue mission, Richard Stanton, as an alternative rescue option in case of more flooding.

With engineers from SpaceX and The Boring Company, and using a Falcon 9 liquid oxygen transfer tube, the mini submarine was built in less than 8 hours and was delivered to the rescue team in Thailand. At the time of its arrival, more than half of the children had already been rescued using alternate means. Although the rescue team opted against using the mini submarine, Musk received the Order of the Direkgunabhorn by the King of Thailand in March 2019, for his involvement.

After the rescue, a British cave explorer who had played a key role in the rescue, and who had been studying the area for six years prior to the incident, criticized the mini submarine, calling it a public relations stunt. In a series of tweets, Musk retaliated by saying that the device was functional and would have worked, and referred to Vernon Unsworth, the caver, as 'pedo guy'. The tweets were later deleted, and Musk apologized, although he later accused Unsworth of marrying a Thai child bride in an email.

Unsworth filed a defamation suit against Musk in September 2019 at the Los Angeles federal court. Court proceedings began in December 2019, with Unsworth seeking $190 million in damages. The jury returned with a verdict in favor of Musk and determined that he was not liable.

Chapter 6: To the Future and Beyond

If something is important enough, even if the odds are against you, you should still do it even if the odds are not in your favor. – Elon Musk

Musk has always had the future in his sights. From his early days with what is now PayPal, to his determination to make human beings a multi-planet species, he has always thought ahead. Some of his predictions have been spot on, while others have widely missed the mark.

Luckily, Musk heads up a variety of companies that will play a crucial role in making his dreams a reality. For self-driving electric vehicles, he has Tesla, which also aids in bringing renewable energy solutions to the fore. SpaceX was created to make humans a multi-planet species. While The Boring Company will revolutionize transportation, OpenAI will play a part in creating responsible artificial intelligence, and Neuralink will assist in augmenting the human brain.

Despite the fact that the COVID-19 pandemic caused industry to slow down, Musk is still going full steam ahead with his visions for the future.

Cars of the Future

Tesla has been thriving in the last few years with plans to build additional factories in Texas and Germany to meet customer needs. Since 2020, its share price has quadrupled, making Tesla the most valuable car manufacturer in the world.

Electric vehicles are expected to boom with the ever-increasing fuel price. Both France and Great Britain have plans to ban the use of petrol and diesel vehicles by 2040. The average American spends approximately $3,000 on fuel per year, while transportation businesses spend upward of $200,000 on fuel per vehicle. Although Tesla vehicles currently rely on the grid for power, the move to fully electric vehicles is almost certain.

Musk has spoken of self-driving vehicles in the past, sometimes to the detriment of Tesla. Tesla is, however, continuously developing their self-driving technology. All four Tesla models are currently equipped with 8 external cameras, 12 sensors and a radar that assist the driver with self-parking and summoning.

There have been a number of safety concerns with regards to self-driving technology, along with the regulatory approval that is required. In 2018, a vehicle in a fatal crash was using Tesla's autopilot system. The National Highway Traffic Safety Administration launched an official investigation into the system in early 2021, after three vehicles crashed using the system.

Tesla's road into the future may be rocky. There has been wide speculation with regards to the company's profitability, and the ability to sustain it. In the US, tax breaks for those purchasing Tesla electric vehicles have ceased, causing a potential downturn in buyer demand.

China is a source of contention for Tesla as well. The Chinese government has banned Tesla vehicles from entering military premises and strategic facilities due to security concerns over the cameras installed on the vehicles, citing that the vehicles have the potential for a national security leak. This is of great concern to Tesla as China accounted for almost one third of all Tesla deliveries in 2020. Musk responded to the claims by stating that any data sourced from the cameras would be held in strictest confidence.

Tesla's recent excursion into the world of cryptocurrency remains to be decided as a success or failure. In February 2021, Tesla purchased $1.5 billion in Bitcoin and announced that the cryptocurrency would be accepted as payment for their vehicles.

A Robot Butler in Every Home

The development process for self-driving vehicles led to Musk realizing that creating artificial intelligence for a vehicle was a natural springboard to creating AI for humanoid robots. As of April 2022, Musk stated that the only missing factors in creating humanoid robots are fine-tuning real world intelligence and ramping up production, two areas where Tesla has excelled. Musk believes that the development of humanoid robots will be "bigger than the car".

OpenAI, where Musk is no longer a board member due to his increased commitment at Tesla, has stated that its mission is to ensure that artificial general intelligence (AGI) —by which they mean highly autonomous systems that outperform humans at most economically valuable work— benefits all of humanity.

At first, the humanoid robots will be put to use in areas where work is repetitive and dangerous, with the first prototypes expected within 2022, and a ready-for-market product within the following two years. Musk is, however, highly concerned that humanoid robots could become hyper-intelligent, leading to a dystopian situation. The fear is twofold; that artificial intelligence will unintentionally cause harm to humans and that it will intentionally cause harm to humans.

Musk predicts that by 2040, there will be more robots than people on the planet. His workaround for this is to prohibit updating the robot's software automatically, instead opting for manual updates by the user. He also believes that AI is the one field that requires intense regulation to prevent a situation where robots become autonomous.

Musk believes that in the next 20 years or so, it will be commonplace for people to have a robot in their homes to take care of things like cooking and cleaning. The humanoid robot butlers would cost less than a car, due to the incremental advances in technology as production improves.

Colonizing the Red Planet

You need to live in a dome initially, but over time you could terraform Mars to look like Earth and eventually walk around outside without anything on... So, it's a fixer-upper of a planet. – Elon Musk

According to Musk, leaving humanity as a single-planet species is a surefire path to extinction. An extinction event, either a grand-scale natural disaster or the rise of superhuman artificial intelligence, will cause the human race to cease to exist if we do not make it a priority to explore space and begin colonizing.

SpaceX was created with this vision in mind. Eliminating other planets as potential hosts for humans, Musk has decided that Mars is the best option. The Martian day is only slightly longer than one Earth day, the temperatures are not as extreme as other planets, and the landmass is similar to that of Earth. Musk believes that it is possible to warm up Mars' surface temperature, creating a thick atmosphere and oceans. He has also stated that with some adjustments, it would be possible to grow plants on the planet.

To date, the high cost of building and launching spacecraft have been the main hindrance to accelerated space exploration and colonization. SpaceX has, however, been able to design and build reusable launch rockets, which will greatly lower the costs of launching to space.

SpaceX has been hard at work to bring down the costs related to space travel and will continue to do so into the future. SpaceX has succeeded in creating reusable rocket technology. The next steps in paving the way to colonizing Mars include developing technologies to refuel while in orbit and creating a suitable fuel source on Mars itself. SpaceX is currently working on developing Methalox, a combination of methane and oxygen.

SpaceX has launched a number of civilians into space thus far, igniting the curiosity of those not yet able to afford such a trip. Musk hopes that by continuing to do so, others will become inspired to sign up for future launches.

SpaceX began developing Starship, a spacecraft capable of transporting 100 people, in 2021. Plans for launching in early 2022 have been moved out, with Starship's first orbital flight scheduled to launch from Boca Chica, Texas, in June 2022. With additional orbital flights planned for 2022 through to 2024, it is expected that the first flight to Mars will take place in 2026. Musk fully believes that the colonization of Mars will be well under way by 2032.

Internet Access For All

Starlink is a project run by SpaceX, which aims at providing internet access to all people, even those in rural communities, around the world. The idea is to go where earthbound networks have been unable to go. The idea of satellite internet is not a new one, with the first companies founded in the 1990's aiming to create a constellation of satellites that would beam the internet down onto earth. Due to the cost implications involved, all of those companies failed and declared bankruptcy.

Starlink has been able to get cost margins down due to SpaceX's development of reusable launch rockets. Starlink is also aiming at providing greater bandwidth in a shorter amount of time compared to the attempts in the 1990's.

By March 2021, Starlink had launched over 1,000 satellites, exceeding the minimum of 800 that would be required for the network to be functional. The Federal Communications Commission (FCC) has stated that 2,400 of Starlink's satellites must be launched by March 2024 as they are reserving a band of telecommunications spectrum specifically for Starlink.

SpaceX is also required to provide a detailed plan on how space debris from deteriorated satellites will be dealt with. The FCC has highlighted a problem with space junk, with approximately 6,000 tons of material in Earth's low orbit, and wants to ensure that SpaceX and Starlink are not contributors to the problem.

Starlink is currently available in the US, UK, and Canada, with plans of expanding to South Africa, Japan, Mexico, Germany, and Austria. Starlink's program has essentially resuscitated the drive for satellite internet, with competitors like Amazon and Apple also gaining approval to create their own constellations of satellites.

Drawing Power from the Sun

SolarCity and the use of renewable energy has long been a passion of Musk's. With the decreasing costs associated with the installation of solar panels, it is becoming more and more affordable to do so, creating a greater demand in the market. Combine that with the high cost of fossil fuels, and the predicted trajectory for SolarCity is almost a sure thing.

There have, however, been growing concerns with regards to the roll out of the Solar Roof, SolarCity's name for their solar panels. Claims by Musk in 2018 that hundreds of homes had Solar Roof installed were misleading and SolarCity rectified the statement by adding that Musk had included homes still scheduled for installation and those that were partially installed.

SolarCity expanded the availability of the Solar Roof to include 25 states in the US and sales increased drastically. In February 2020, Musk announced that SolarCity would be expanding into the international market, although this has yet to come to fruition.

Connecting Human Brains to Computers

While Musk's other ventures are large-scale, Neuralink takes things to a microscopic level, going into the human brain by building a brain-computer interface. Musk recently described the interface as "a FitBit in your skull".

Musk believes that enhancing our cognitive functioning is the only way that humans will be able to keep up with the advancement of artificial intelligence, and that without it, we will end up in the dystopian future he so greatly fears. By connecting humans and computers, we would be able to carry out certain tasks by merely thinking about them.

The inspiration for the brain-computer interface stems from veterans who have lost limbs in combat. The Defense Advanced Research Projects Agency's (DARPA) Revolutionizing Prosthetics program has created artificial limbs with brain implants, allowing the wearer to control the artificial limb, to an extent, through brain activity. To simply lift a cup of coffee uses millions of neurons, and currently the technology is not able to process the volume of neural activity taking place.

This is where Neuralink comes in; researching and developing an interface that is able to transmit the full suite of neurological activity taking place for any one action, and bridging gaps between brain and body. Human trials are expected to take place in late 2022.

Hyperspeed Underground Travel

The concept of transporting people in underground tunnels at high speeds was first proposed in 1828 by an Englishman named George Medhurst. While underground railway systems currently exist around the world, Musk introduced the world to the Hyperloop idea in 2012. Dubbing it the fifth mode of transport, Musk elaborated that travel would take place in a low-pressure tube, with passengers in a pod-like capsule, supported by air and powered by a magnetic linear accelerator.

Unfortunately, the technology is not yet ready. Although The Boring Company is able to dig the tunnels, the development of Hyperloop technology has not kept up. Despite the setback, Musk has stated that construction will begin in the next few years.

Easing Above-Ground Traffic Congestion

The Boring Company will continue to expand the tunnels beneath Las Vegas to include McCarran International Airport, Allegiant Stadium, downtown Las Vegas, and eventually to reach Los Angeles.

The Dugout Loop, which aims to connect East Hollywood and Dodger Stadium in Los Angeles, remains under review by the Los Angeles Bureau of Engineering. The East Coast Loop, connecting Washington DC and Baltimore, is also under review.

Despite setbacks in gaining approval for the two above mentioned projects, Musk believes that the creation of loops within cities will greatly benefit Tesla, as plans show that the tunnels will be for the exclusive use of electric vehicles. The Boring Company's efforts will also be essential for the Hyperloop project, as the boring technology evolves, and digging efficiency improves. Finally, SpaceX will also benefit from TBC. With the view of colonizing Mars, tunneling may have to take place on the planet, as people may need to live underground due to inhospitable conditions.

Conclusion

Life needs to be more than just solving problems every day.
You need to wake up and be excited about the future.
– Elon Musk

Elon Musk is seen as a revolutionary inventor, a big dreamer, and an eccentric individual. He may not always be understood, especially by the general public, but he has definitely captured their attention.

With his passion, drive, and intelligence, he has been able to pursue his ultimate dream; enriching the world through technological advances.

His achievements so far have been many, but he is showing no signs of slowing down! If things go to plan, he will continue to have a huge impact on life on Earth (and Mars!) for many years to come!

References

8 Industries Being Disrupted By Elon Musk And His Companies. (2018). CB Insights

Research. https://www.cbinsights.com/research/report/elon-musk-companies-disruption/

About OpenAI. (2015, December 11). OpenAI. https://openai.com/about/#:~:text=OpenAI

Ahead of 2022, Elon Musk is already wondering about "futuristic" 2032 & his space journey

to Mars. (2021, December 14). *The Economic Times.*

https://economictimes.indiatimes.com/magazines/panache/ahead-of-2022-elon-musk-is-

already-wondering-about-futuristic-2032-and-his-space-journey-to-

mars/articleshow/88253668.cms

Arcand, R. (2019, March 31). *Elon Musk Drops Surprise Rap Single "RIP Harambe."* SPIN.

https://www.spin.com/2019/03/elon-musk-drops-rap-single-rip-harambe/

Bang Showbiz. (2022, May 22). *Who is Talulah Riley, Elon Musk's second wife who divorced*

him twice? Www.iol.co.za. https://www.iol.co.za/lifestyle/love-sex/relationships/who-is-

talulah-riley-elon-musks-second-wife-who-divorced-him-twice-29460ab6-ba23-5cf9-9d77-

7500398a34f6

Brandom, R. (2020, April 29). *Elon Musk is dangerously wrong about the novel coronavirus.*

The Verge. https://www.theverge.com/2020/4/29/21241180/elon-musk-coronavirus-

conspiracy-misinformation-tesla

Dom Galeon. (2017, November 21). *Here's a List of Everything Elon Musk Says He'll Do by*

2030. Futurism; Futurism. https://futurism.com/heres-list-everything-elon-musk-2030

Duffy, C. (2022, April 5). *Elon Musk to join Twitter's board.* CNN.

https://edition.cnn.com/2022/04/05/tech/elon-musk-twitter-board/index.html

Elon Musk Quotes (Author of Elon Musk). (n.d.). Www.goodreads.com.

https://www.goodreads.com/author/quotes/7221234.Elon_Musk

Elon Musk talks Twitter, Tesla and how his brain works — live at TED2022. (2022, April 14).

Www.youtube.com.

https://www.youtube.com/watch?v=cdZZpaB2kDM&t=767s&ab_channel=TED

Elon Musk: The future we're building -- and boring | TED. (2017, May 17).

Www.youtube.com. https://www.youtube.com/watch?v=zIwLWfaAg-

8&t=10m29s&ab_channel=TED

Etherington, D. (2020, January 31). *Elon Musk just dropped an EDM track on SoundCloud*.

TechCrunch. https://techcrunch.com/2020/01/31/elon-musk-just-dropped-an-edm-track-

on-soundcloud/

FAQ - The Giving Pledge. (n.d.). Giving Pledge. https://www.givingpledge.org/faq/

Farivar, C. (2021, January 8). *Fort Lauderdale officials say Elon Musk's new tunnel to the

beach can't come fast enough*. NBC News. https://www.nbcnews.com/tech/tech-news/urban-

tunnels-musk-s-boring-co-draw-industry-skepticism-n1269677

Ginsberg, L. (2017, June 16). *Elon Musk thinks life on earth will go extinct, and is putting

most of his fortune toward colonizing Mars*. CNBC.

https://www.cnbc.com/2017/06/16/elon-musk-colonize-mars-before-extinction-event-on-

earth.html

Goldstein, M., & Flitter, E. (2020, June 23). *Tesla Chief Elon Musk Is Sued by S.E.C. in Move

That Could Oust Him - The New York Times*. Web.archive.org.

https://web.archive.org/web/20200623023744/https://www.nytimes.com/2018/09/27/busi

ness/elon-musk-sec-lawsuit-tesla.html

Grebenyuk, Y. (2022, May 31). *Elon Musk and Amber Heard's Relationship Timeline: The

Way They Were*. Us Weekly. https://www.usmagazine.com/celebrity-news/pictures/elon-

musk-and-amber-heards-relationship-timeline/may-2022/

Grush, L. (2020, August 25). *The Air Force is determining "the appropriate process" for Elon

Musk smoking pot - The Verge*. Web.archive.org.

https://web.archive.org/web/20200825132601/https://www.theverge.com/2018/9/7/17833

208/elon-musk-air-force-pot-smoking-investigation

Harris, M. (2019, January 24). *How Elon Musk's secretive foundation hands out his billions*.

The Guardian; The Guardian. https://www.theguardian.com/technology/2019/jan/23/how-

elon-musks-secretive-foundation-benefits-his-own-family

Hiltzik, M. (2022, May 1). *Twitter, Elon Musk and free-speech absolutism*. The Seattle Times.

https://www.seattletimes.com/opinion/twitter-elon-musk-and-free-speech-absolutism/

Lopatto, E. (2018, June 10). *I have a Boring Company Not-A-Flamethrower*. The Verge. https://www.theverge.com/2018/6/10/17445838/boring-company-flamethrower-elon-musk-tweets-party

Mankarious, S.-G., Chacón, M., Duffy, C., & Thorbecke, C. (2022, April 29). *Here's what Elon Musk has tweeted over the years ... about Twitter*. Www.cnn.com. https://edition.cnn.com/interactive/2022/04/business/elon-musk-tweets-twitter/index.html

McHugh, R. (2022, May 20). *SpaceX employee said Elon Musk exposed himself to her - documents show. She got R4m for her silence*. Businessinsider. https://www.businessinsider.co.za/spacex-paid-250000-to-a-flight-attendant-who-accused-elon-musk-of-sexual-misconduct-2022-5?r=US&IR=T

Musk Foundation. (n.d.). www.muskfoundation.org. http://www.muskfoundation.org/

Musk Foundation. (2019). Influencewatch.org. https://www.influencewatch.org/non-profit/musk-foundation/

Musk, J. (2010, September 10). *"I Was a Starter Wife": Inside America's Messiest Divorce*. Marie Claire. https://www.marieclaire.com/sex-love/a5380/millionaire-starter-wife/

Orlandini, G. (2022, January 27). *What Elon Musk's Private Life Is Really Like*. Grunge.com. https://www.grunge.com/749750/what-elon-musks-private-life-is-really-like/#:~:text=Elon%20Musk%20has%20been%20married

Paleja, A. (2021, September 23). *Musk's Boring Company Announces Not-a-Boring Competition Winner*. Interesting Engineering. https://interestingengineering.com/musks-boring-company-announces-not-a-boring-competition-winner

Petridis, A. (2020, June 21). *Elon Musk's new EDM single reviewed – "Bringing erectile dysfunction to the masses!" | Music | The Guardian*. Web.archive.org. https://web.archive.org/web/20200621190025/https://www.theguardian.com/music/2020/jan/31/elon-musk-edm-artist-first-track-dont-doubt-ur-vibe

Quotes about Elon Musk. (n.d.). BrainyQuote. Retrieved June 3, 2022, from https://www.brainyquote.com/topics/elon-musk-quotes#:~:text=Elon%20Musk%20is%20a%20very

Rai, S. (2022, April 25). *Republicans praise Musk's Twitter acquisition; Democrats skeptical.* The Hill. https://thehill.com/news/house/3462806-republicans-praise-musks-twitter-acquisition-democrats-skeptical/

Reed, E. (2020, February 4). *History of Tesla: timeline and facts.* TheStreet. https://www.thestreet.com/technology/history-of-tesla-15088992

Regalado, A. (2020, August 30). *Elon Musk's Neuralink is neuroscience theater | MIT Technology Review.* Web.archive.org. https://web.archive.org/web/20220118052441/https://www.technologyreview.com/2020/08/30/1007786/elon-musks-neuralink-demo-update-neuroscience-theater/

Robinson, N. J. (2021, April 7). *Surely We Can Do Better Than Elon Musk.* Current Affairs. https://www.currentaffairs.org/2021/04/surely-we-can-do-better-than-elon-musk

Roumeliotis, G. (2022, April 26). Musk gets Twitter for $44 billion, to cheers and fears of "free speech" plan. *Reuters.* https://www.reuters.com/technology/exclusive-twitter-set-accept-musks-best-final-offer-sources-2022-04-25/

Sato, M. (2022, April 14). *Buying Twitter "is not a way to make money," says Musk in TED interview.* The Verge. https://www.theverge.com/2022/4/14/23025343/elon-musk-twitter-takeover-ted-talk-quote-stock-buyout

Schwedel, H. (2021, September 27). *A Brief, Weird History of Elon Musk and Grimes' Brief, Weird Relationship.* Slate Magazine. https://slate.com/human-interest/2021/09/elon-musk-and-grimes-relationship-a-brief-weird-history.html

Smith, A. (2022, April 4). *The strangest things Elon Musk has ever done on Twitter.* The Independent. https://www.independent.co.uk/tech/elon-musk-twitter-history-tweets-b2050576.html

Srivastava, I. (2022, May 18). *Amber Heard and Elon Musk: A timeline of their relationship.* Www.dailyo.in. https://www.dailyo.in/variety/amber-heard-johnny-depp-elon-musk-timeline/story/1/35917.html

Statt, N. (2018, January 29). *California politician will seek sale ban on Elon Musk's Boring Company flamethrower.* The Verge. https://www.theverge.com/2018/1/29/16948090/elon-musk-boring-company-flamethrower-california-sales-ban-miguel-santiago

Stewart, E. (2018, September 8). *Tesla's Elon Musk smokes weed on Joe Rogan podcast, havoc ensues.* Vox; Vox. https://www.vox.com/business-and-finance/2018/9/8/17834910/elon-musk-joe-rogan-podcast-tesla-stock

Strauss, N. (2017, November 15). *Elon Musk: Inventor's Plans for Outer Space, Cars, Finding Love – Rolling Stone.* Rollingstone.com; Rolling Stone. https://www.rollingstone.com/culture/culture-features/elon-musk-the-architect-of-tomorrow-120850/

Vance, A. (2015). *Elon Musk : Tesla, SpaceX, and the quest for a fantastic future.* Ecco.

Weiler, L. (2020, May 6). *Elon Musk Married Talulah Riley Twice Before Divorcing Her for Good.* Showbiz Cheat Sheet. https://www.cheatsheet.com/entertainment/elon-musk-married-talulah-riley-twice-before-divorcing-her-for-good.html/

Wolfe, S. (2018, August 21). *Elon Musk and his girlfriend Grimes could be on the rocks — here's a look inside their relationship and how it all started.* Businessinsider. https://www.businessinsider.co.za/elon-musk-girlfriend-grimes-relationship-photos-2018-8?r=US&IR=T

Wong, J. C. (2019, December 5). *Elon Musk trial: Vernon Unsworth says entrepreneur's tweets "humiliated" him.* The Guardian. https://www.theguardian.com/technology/2019/dec/04/elon-musk-trial-twitter-thai-rescue

Milton Keynes UK
Ingram Content Group UK Ltd.
UKHW010653140324
439439UK00015B/1743